YAY, US!

MADE FOR YOU BY...

THIS BOOK IS DEDICATED EXCLUSIVELY,

SOLELY, UTTERLY,

COMPLETELY, WHOLLY,

ENTIRELY TO

....

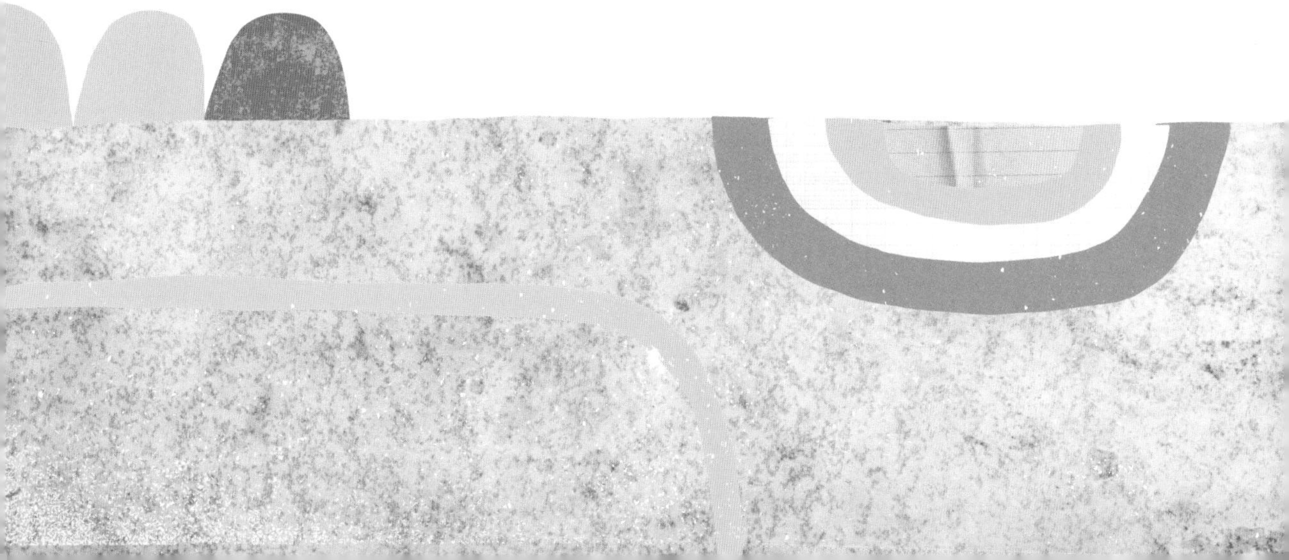

WE'VE BEEN

FOR

YEARS!

BUT REALLY,
I FEEL LIKE
I'VE KNOWN YOU
SINCE

________.

THE
FIRST
TIME
WE MET,

IT WAS ____________

OUTSIDE AND MY

HEART WAS POUNDING!

OUR...

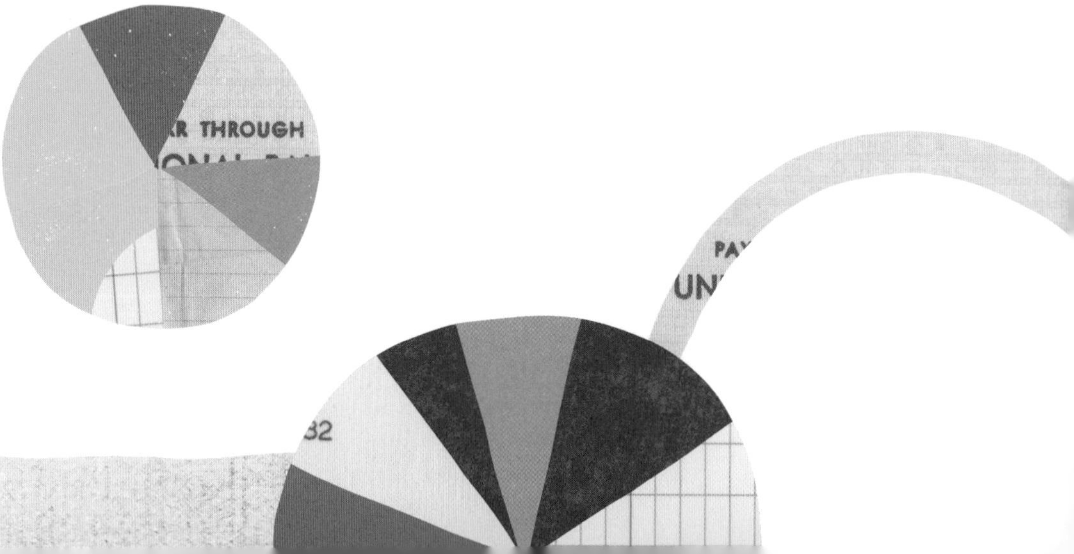

....

IS PROBABLY MY MOST
FAVORITE THING ABOUT US!
ON A SCALE OF 1 TO 10,
WE'RE A .... FOR SURE.

IF I SAW A SHOOTING STAR...

I WOULD WISH THAT YOU & I WOULD NEVER

____

BUT IF I SAW A

DINOSAUR

WALKING DOWN

THE ROAD...

HEADED STRAIGHT
TOWARD US,
I'D PROBABLY

ONE DAY

THEY'LL MAKE A
MONUMENT OF US.
IT WILL BE MADE OF
GOLD AND RUBIES
AND DIAMONDS AND
STAND 12 FEET HIGH.

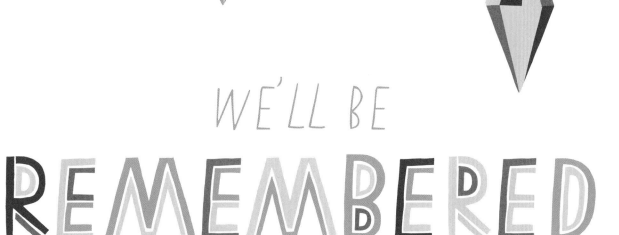

WE'LL BE

REMEMBERED

BY ALL FOR BEING

....

AND ....

AND ....

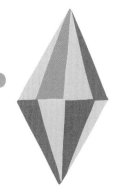

WHEN I WRITE THAT

BEST-SELLING

BOOK ABOUT US,

IT WILL BE TITLED

______________________.

AND IF SHAKESPEARE

WROTE A

PLAY ABOUT US,

HE'D CALL IT

BEFORE I KNEW YOU

I HAD TO

ALONE.

BUT NOW
YOU'RE MY GO-TO
EVERY TIME

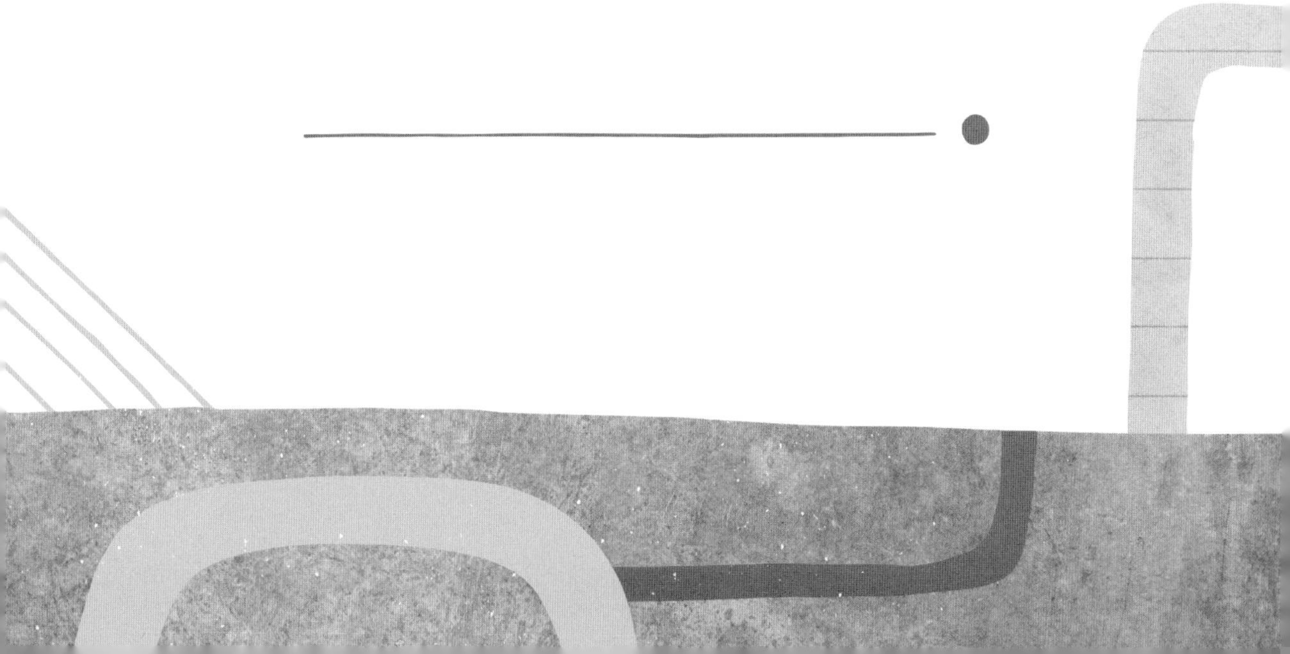

I COMPLETELY UNDERSTAND WHAT WE WOULD NEED TO SURVIVE FOR A YEAR ON A DESERTED ISLAND!

YOU WOULD CRY WITHOUT YOUR ______________________.

I WOULD PASS OUT WITHOUT MY ______________________.

AND WE WOULD SELL OUR SOULS (OKAY, PROBABLY NOT) FOR ONE MORE PIECE OF

______________________.

(OKAY, MAYBE WE WOULD.)

32

REMEMBER

THAT TIME YOU AND I

______________________________?

IT WAS THE

(CIRCLE ALL THAT APPLY)

TIME WE'VE SHARED TOGETHER!

SILLIEST	MOST MEMORABLE	WORST	MOST VICTORIOUS
FUNNIEST	BRAVEST	COLDEST	CUTEST
BESTEST	MOST OBNOXIOUS	HOTTEST	GRUMPIEST
FUNNEST	SCARIEST	GREATEST	HAPPIEST

JACK WAS

NIMBLE AND QUICK,
BUT NOT AS MUCH AS US

THAT TIME WE

______________________ .

WE CAN WATCH

TOGETHER OVER AND OVER
WITHOUT EVER GETTING
TIRED OF IT!

SINCE
WE
MET,

I BET

BETWEEN THE TWO OF US,
WE'VE EXCHANGED APPROXIMATELY

______ PHONE CALLS

______ TEXT MESSAGES

______ HANDWRITTEN NOTES

______ VIDEOS

______ CARRIER PIGEONS

______ SONGS

IF I HAD

ONE MONTH

OFF OF WORK

AND A

MILLION DOLLARS,

FIRST I'D WANT TO TRAVEL TO

____________ WITH YOU,

AND THEN I THINK WE SHOULD

____

WITH THE REST OF THE CASH!

SOME PEOPLE SAY

THEY'RE SURPRISED
WE GET ALONG SO WELL
BECAUSE I'M REALLY

____

AND YOU'RE QUITE

______________________.

WE DON'T LISTEN THOUGH!
BECAUSE SOME THINGS
JUST DON'T MAKE SENSE!
BUT WE DO, BECAUSE
YOU ARE PERFECTLY

____

AND I AM EXACTLY

______________________.

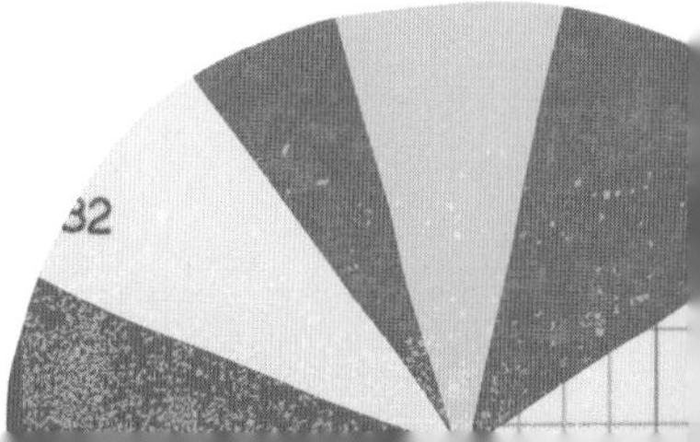

THAT TIME

YOU

SCARED THE HECK OUT OF ME!

BUT I'LL ALWAYS BE YOUR

WINGPERSON,

EVEN WHEN

______________.

NO ONE ENJOYS MY

____

THE WAY YOU DO.

AND

I'M PRETTY SURE

NO ONE APPRECIATES YOUR

____

THE WAY I DO.

YOU CAN PROTECT ME
FROM VAMPIRES AND
ZOMBIES,

BUT I'LL PROTECT
YOU FROM
________ AND ________.
OUR SAFE WORD
WOULD BE
....

WHEN I

WENT THROUGH

________________,

MY WORLD

TURNED UPSIDE DOWN.

BUT YOU

AND I LEARNED
TO LIVE RIGHT SIDE UP
AGAIN.

MY NOSE

WOULD GROW
SO LONG
IF I TRIED
TO CONVINCE
ANYONE THAT
WE ARE

ROSES ARE RED
VIOLETS ARE BLUE

WE WOULD

....

IF WE ATTEMPTED
KUNG FU.

DESPITE
THE LATE
HOUR,

AFTER MIDNIGHT
WE WOULD STILL

____

AND ______________________,

OR MAYBE JUST

______________________________,

BUT PROBABLY

______________________________.

I CAN'T

BELIEVE

WE USED TO

....!

A PERFECT MEMENTO OF US WOULD BE

A TRUSTED
SECRET BETWEEN US
THAT WILL GO
TO OUR GRAVES IS

(MAYBE YOU SHOULD
SCRIBBLE OVER THAT ONCE
YOU READ THAT PAGE!!)

WE

DEFINITELY LOOK STUPID
WHEN WE

________________________,

BUT I WOULDN'T WANT TO

____

WITH ANYONE ELSE!

IF WE STARTED A SECRET SOCIETY IT WOULD BE ABOUT

....

AND WE'D CALL IT

....

AND THE FIRST PERSON WE'D INVITE TO JOIN WOULD BE

....

OR

YOU AND I

WAKE UP AND WE'RE IN JAIL.

I THINK WE UNDOUBTEDLY

____

TO GET THROWN IN THERE.

WE'LL

PROBABLY END UP

(CIRCLE TWO THAT ARE MOST LIKELY)

LAUGHING UNTIL WE PEE OUR PANTS

DYING FROM EMBARRASSMENT

SWEET TALKING THE GUARD TO LET US OUT

FINDING A WAY TO ESCAPE

CALLING ______________

ASKING IF THEY HAVE ANY______________

YOU DON'T

JUDGE ME FOR

....

AND

I DON'T

JUDGE YOU FOR

....

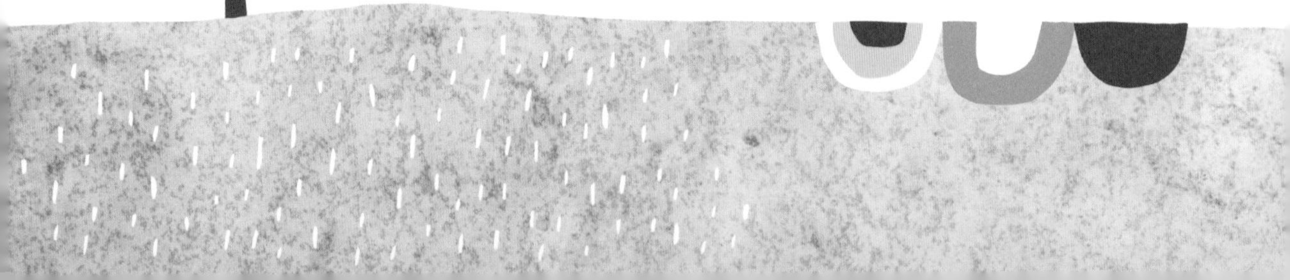

REMEMBER WHEN
THE WHOLE NEIGHBORHOOD
HATED US FOR SINGING

WAY TOO LOUD
OUT OUR CAR WINDOWS?!

THE BEST/WORST
(CIRCLE ONE)
PRACTICAL JOKE
WE EVER PLAYED
WAS ON

AND

THEY THOUGHT

IT WAS SUPER

I'VE NEVER TRIED

BEFORE.

BUT

WITH YOU,

I TRIED IT AND
ABSOLUTELY,
WITHOUT A DOUBT,
DEFINITELY

________________ IT!

YOU AND I

GO TO AN ANTIQUE STORE.

WE'RE MOST LIKELY GOING TO BUY

(CIRCLE ALL THAT APPLY)

- JEWELRY
- A HUGE ________
- WEIRD-LOOKING CHRISTMAS ORNAMENTS
- FIRST-EDITION BOOKS
- A PAINTING (OR MAYBE 2 OR 3)
- POSTCARDS
- OLD KEYS
- A RECORD PLAYER
- ANTIQUE PHOTOGRAPHS
- FURNITURE
- OLD TOYS
- FIVE ________
- A GUITAR

MAKES US

ROLL OUR EYES

EVERY SINGLE TIME

WE HEAR IT.

REMEMBER

WHEN WE THOUGHT

....

WAS A GOOD/BAD (CIRCLE ONE) IDEA??

YEP.

IT'S A TOSS-UP.

CAN'T DECIDE IF WE ARE

____

OR ________________ .

IF OUR TIME

TOGETHER WERE TO BE NARRATED,

I WOULD CHOOSE ____________

AS THE NARRATOR.

AND

YOU WOULD PROBABLY CHOOSE

....

BECAUSE THEY'RE JUST SO

....

THERE ARE

SOME THINGS
I KNOW FOR SURE!

1. IF YOU COULD HAVE A MINIATURE ANIMAL FROM THE ZOO AS A PET, YOU'D CHOOSE A ________________.
AND I'D CHOOSE ________________.
2. IF YOU WERE AN ARTICLE OF CLOTHING YOU'D BE ________________________.
3. THE MOVIE ______________ SCARED US TO DEATH!
4. WE CRIED TOGETHER WHEN

____.
5. AND WE LAUGHED TOGETHER WHEN

____.

IF IT WERE OUR **LAST DAY** ON EARTH, IT WOULD CONSIST OF:

1. ______________________________

2. ______________________________

3. ______________________________

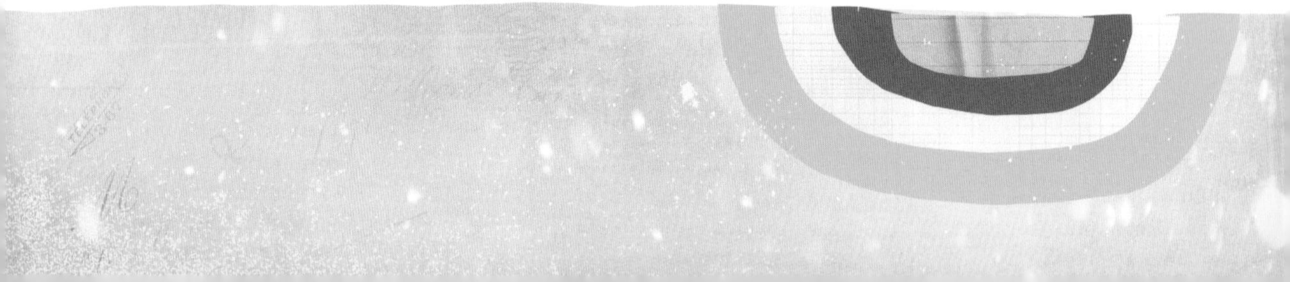

A PICTURE PAINTS A THOUSAND WORDS,

AND OUR PIECE OF ART WOULD INCLUDE A

______________________________,

A ______________________________,

AND A ______________________________.

A LLAMACORN IS A

COMBINATION OF A LLAMA AND A UNICORN.

JUST AS UNIQUE,

YOU AND ME AND ME AND YOU AND BOTH OF US ARE A COMBINATION OF

________ AND ________.

YOU

EARNED THIS BOOK
BECAUSE OF THE WAY YOU

AND I'LL ALWAYS BELIEVE
THAT YOU DESERVE
NOTHING LESS THAN
EVERYTHING BEAUTIFUL.

I THINK

WE'RE ....

PERIOD.

FULL STOP.

END OF SENTENCE.

BECAUSE WITHOUT YOU
I WOULDN'T BE ME.
AND MAYBE WITHOUT ME
YOU WOULDN'T BE YOU.
AND WITHOUT US...
WELL THAT'S TOO SCARY
TO THINK ABOUT!
YOU'RE THE PEANUT BUTTER
TO MY JELLY. THE FLIP
TO MY FLOP. THE SHAKE
TO MY BAKE AND THE
SPRINKLES TO MY ICE CREAM.

BUT MOST

IMPORTANTLY,

YOU'LL ALWAYS BE

THE ______________

TO MY ______________.

GIBBS SMITH
TO ENRICH AND INSPIRE HUMANKIND

24 23 22 21 20 5 4 3 2 1

Published by
Gibbs Smith
P.O. Box 667
Layton, Utah 84041

1.800.835.4993 orders
www.gibbs-smith.com

Designed by Nicole LaRue

Printed and bound in China
Gibbs Smith books are printed on either recycled, 100% post-consumer waste, FSC-certified papers or on paper produced from sustainable PEFC-certified forest/controlled wood source. Learn more at www.pefc.org.

ISBN: 978-1-4236-5416-2